My First Book about Rabbits

Amazing Animal Books
Children's Picture Books

By Molly Davidson
Mendon Cottage Books

JD-Biz Publishing

Read More Amazing Animal Books

Purchase at Amazon.com

Download Free Books!
http://MendonCottageBooks.com

Table of Contents

Introduction

Rabbits live in the wild and many are kept as pets.

They are very cute and cuddly, and enjoy being petted.

Many animals, like wolves and foxes, eat rabbits.

What are rabbits?

Another name for a rabbit is a bunny, but a bunny is usually a younger rabbit.

Rabbits live everywhere in the World, except for Antarctica.

A boy rabbit is called a buck, a girl is called a doe, and a baby is known as a kitten or kit.

A group of rabbits is called a warren.

Before rabbits were kept as pets, they were eaten by the poor, and it was a sport to hunt rabbits if you were royalty.

What do rabbits eat?

Rabbits only eat plants, no meat, like grass, weeds, and other green plants.

An albino rabbit eating

Rabbits like to graze, which means eat a little bit of food many times per day.

They have two pair of front teeth; one set is in front of the other. Their teeth are perfect for chewing up leaves and plants.

You need to be careful, if you have a garden, because rabbits will eat all the vegetables you are growing, and then you won't have any to eat.

What do rabbits look like?

Rabbits have long ears, long back legs, and little paws. They are covered in fur, and they have big eyes.

A lop-eared rabbit

Rabbits can have fur that is brown, black, grey, white, or a mix.

Rabbits have 28 teeth total, humans have 32.

Most rabbits have a fluffy tail that is usually the same color as their fur.

They have five toes on their front paws and only four toes on the back paws.

How do rabbits act?

When rabbits feel threatened, they get aggressive. They will jump, bite, or scratch.

A rabbit in the grass

Rabbits will growl and wag their tails, if they angry or scared.

You will know that a rabbit is happy when it makes squeaky noises.

Rabbits like to live in groups; they do not like to be alone.

Many rabbits sleep with their eyes open to look out for predators.

Their eyes are on the side of their head so they can almost most see in every direction without turning their head.

To warn other rabbits of danger, they will thump their feet hard against the ground.

Baby bunnies (kittens) are born blind and hairless.

Rabbits can run 30 miles per hour (mph) up to 40 mph.

Rabbits as pets

Rabbits are very gentle and loving, so they make great pets.

A rabbit in a cage

Rabbits that are pets need to have fresh food every day, and always have water to drink.

They need to have space to run and exercise. So if their cage isn't big enough, they will need to be let out to go play in the grass or in a larger pen somewhere.

Rabbits like to be outside; they need sunshine and fresh air.

When picking up a rabbit, they like their bums supported, they do not like dangling in the air.

They can get scared easily, make sure to talk to them as you are reaching for them, keep loud noises away from them, and do not run them into a corner.

European Rabbits

European rabbits actually live in Europe, northern Africa, and has been brought to many other places in the World.

Two baby European rabbits

They like to live in groups of no more than 12 rabbits, and they dig deep burrows with many tunnels, so they can live together.

European rabbits like to have their own space, so if another animal tries to take it away from them, they will fight, and they usually win.

They can have babies about every four weeks, and they usually have lots every time they give birth.

Cottontail Rabbits

Cottontails are one of the most numerous (lots of them) kinds of rabbits.

They live all over America, and live in nests they build on the ground.

A cottontail rabbit

They are called cottontails, because their fluffy, white tails look like a white cotton puff.

Volcano Rabbits

The volcano rabbit lives in Mexico, next to four volcanoes.

It is the second smallest kind of rabbit in the world; it barely weighs a pound,

dispale © <u>Wikimedia Commons</u>

Volcano rabbits have been hunted by the Mexicans for many years and they are now endangered.

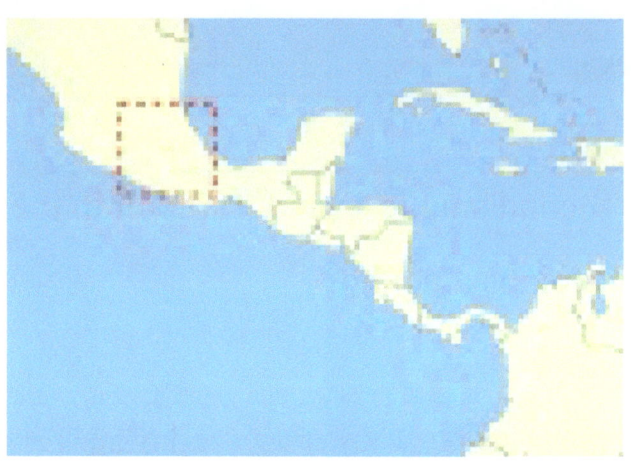

Area where volcano rabbits live

Oona Räisänen © <u>Wikimedia Commons</u>

They come out at night, and live high above sea level.

To warn others of danger they make a high pitched noise.

Pygmy Rabbits

The pygmy rabbit is the smallest rabbit; it weighs a pound or less, and lives in North America.

U.S. Government National Park Service ©

Wikimedia Commons

They live in places with brush, so they can hide, and they are very good at digging burrows, even in the snow.

Amami Rabbits

Amami rabbits are a rare and endangered kind of rabbit that lives on the islands of Japan.

They have shorter ears than most rabbits. They also have short back legs, a bigger body, and smaller eyes; their fur is brown and reddish-brown.

A stamp with a picture of an Amami rabbit on it

The mother will dig a hole for her babies to hide in during the day and then come out at night.

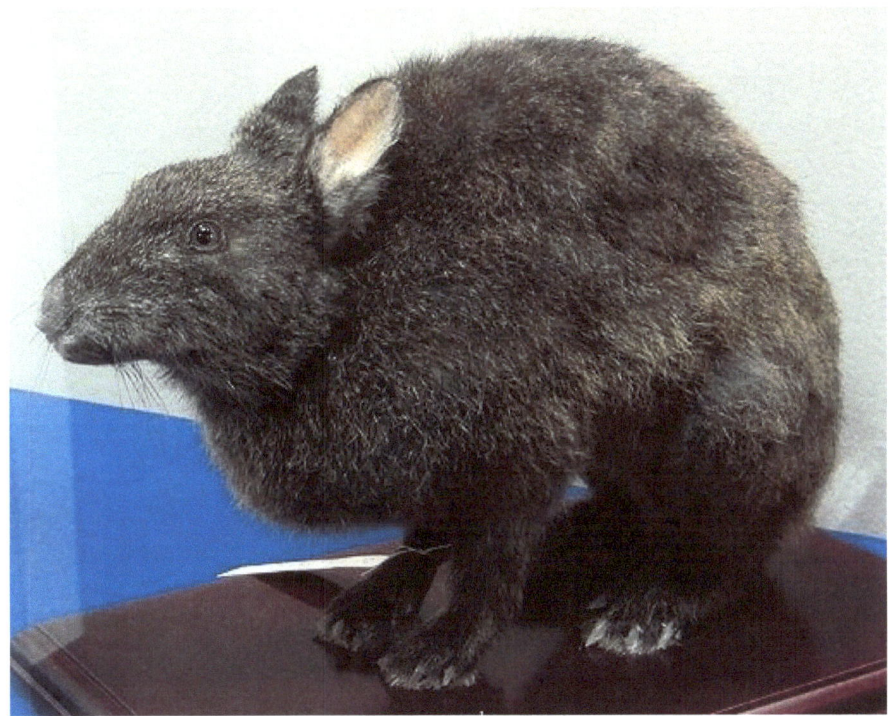

A stuffed Amami rabbit in a museum in Tokyo

Momotarou © <u>Wikimedia Commons</u>

Australian Rabbits

There are no rabbits that are originally from Australia.

© **Wikimedia Commons**

A gentleman from England wanted to hunt rabbits, so he had European rabbits brought to Australia, and he set them free in his backyard.

The problem is no animals in Australia eat rabbits, so there are millions of rabbits now.

They eat many farmers' crops and make many messes.

A sign against rabbit keeping in Australia

Australia has tried to have people hunt them, they tried to build fences, and nothing has worked.

Pikas

Pikas are related to the rabbit, because they make a noise that sounds like a rabbit or a hare.

An American pika on a rock

They live in colder climates in the rocks of the mountains of Europe, Asia, and North America.

They eat the same foods as rabbits and make burrows in the cracks of rocks.

Hares

Hares are a little different from rabbits. They have longer legs, body, and ears, and run faster.

They do not burrow, they build nests.

Jackrabbits are actually a type of hare.

A young hare is called a leveret.

Hares are shy, and do not make very good pets, like rabbits do.

Black Tailed Jackrabbit

Conclusion

Rabbits have been used as food, test animals, zoo animals, and pets. They have been useful to humans in more ways than we can understand.

Rabbits have been around for thousands of years, and are in many folklore stories and myths.

Purchase at Amazon.com
Website http://AmazingAnimalBooks.com

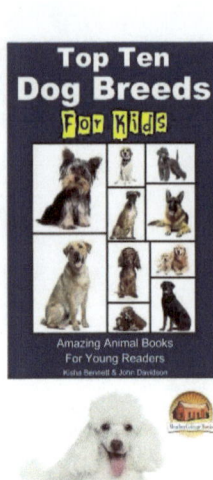

Top Ten Dog Breeds For Kids

Amazing Animal Books For Young Readers

Kisha Bennett & John Davidson

German Shepherds

Dog Books for Kids

K. Bennett

Bulldogs

Dog Books for Kids

K. Bennett

Dachshund

Dog Books for Kids

K. Bennett

Poodles

Dog Books for Kids

K. Bennett

Labrador Retrievers

Dog Books for Kids

K. Bennett

Rottweilers

Dog Books for Kids

K. Bennett

Boxers

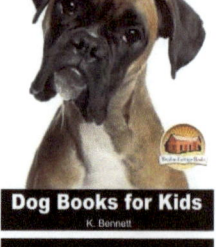

Dog Books for Kids

K. Bennett

Golden Retrievers

Dog Books for Kids

K. Bennett

Puppies

Dog Books For Kids

Amazing Animal Books

By John Davidson

Beagles

Dog Books for Kids

K. Bennett

Yorkshire Terriers

Dog Books for Kids

K. Bennett

Dogs

Top Ten Dog Breeds For Kids

Amazing Animal Books For Young Readers

Zahra Jazeel & John Davidson

Cats For Kids

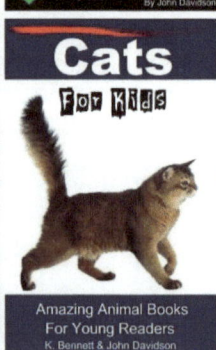

Amazing Animal Books For Young Readers

K. Bennett & John Davidson

Foxes For Kids

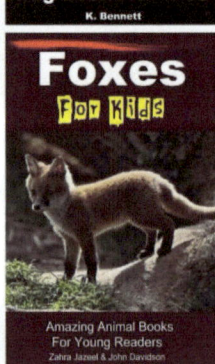

Amazing Animal Books For Young Readers

Zahra Jazeel & John Davidson

Wolves For Kids

Amazing Animal Books For Young Readers

By John Davidson and Virginia Fidler

Our books are available at

1. Amazon.com

2. Barnes and Noble

3. Itunes

4. Kobo

5. Smashwords

6. Google Play Books

Download Free Books!
http://MendonCottageBooks.com

Publisher

JD-Biz Corp

P O Box 374

Mendon, Utah 84325

http://www.jd-biz.com/

www.ingramcontent.com/pod-product-compliance
Lightning Source LLC
Chambersburg PA
CBHW050856290526
45792CB00002B/619